THE BUMP
TWO RONN

A Star Original

This is a selectio
the three books of news items from 'The Two Ronnies' that have already appeared in Star Paperbacks, 'But first the News', 'Nice to be With You Again' and 'In a Packed Programme Tonight'. All the favourites are here and there's also important news of Honest Jack Duggan (bookie and sex maniac) who, when charged with seducing a young lady at Becher's Brook, asked for 26 other fences to be taken into consideration . . .

But the lights are lit. The cameras are ready. With that desk you can't tell if anyone's feet don't touch the ground or if anyone else's stomach does . . . it's time again for 'Good evening . . .'

THE BUMPER BOOK OF THE TWO RONNIES

THE VERY BEST OF THE NEWS

Compiled and edited by Ian Davidson and Peter Vincent

STAR

A STAR BOOK
published by
the Paperback division of
W. H. ALLEN & CO. Ltd

A Star Book
Published in 1978
by the Paperback Division of
W. H. Allen & Co. Ltd
A Howard and Wyndham Company
44 Hill Street, London W1X 8LB

Typesetting by Yale Press Ltd, London SE25
Printed in Great Britain by
Hazell Watson & Viney Ltd,
Aylesbury, Bucks

ISBN 0 352 30249 6

Also featuring the Two Ronnies' dialogue in *Star*

BUT FIRST THE NEWS
NICE TO BE WITH YOU AGAIN
IN A PACKED PROGRAMME
TONIGHT

GOOD EVENING...

Ronnie Corbett: It's nice to be with you again, isn't it Ronnie?

Ronnie Barker: Yes it is and in a packed show tonight we'll be talking to all seven members of the Dublin String Quartet.

RC: And to a masochist who likes nothing better than a cold bath every morning — so he has a warm bath every morning.

RB: And to a man who claims to be such a complete so-and-so that on Father's Day he sends a card addressed to Anon.

RC: And to a Scotsman who was very nearly drowned in the Black Sea while he was filling his fountain pen.

RB: And to a pathetic out-of-work contortionist who says he can no longer make ends meet.

RC: And to an enormously tall boxer who's had to retire from the ring with cauliflower knees.

RB: After that we'll be talking by long distance phone to another Scotsman who found an Australian penny and emigrated.

RC: Then we'll talk to a stereo expert about his favourite breakfast — two bowls of rice crispies ten feet apart.

RB: And we'll talk to the Texas man who made a fortune selling smokeless fuel to Red Indian couples who are not speaking to each other.

RC: And to a famous one-fingered pickpocket who only steals Polo mints.

RB: And then a lady who's a world authority on carpets, an expert on rugs, and not at all bad on lino.

RC: And a hokey cokey champion who's just been disqualified for putting it in when he should have been shaking it all about.

RB: And to a great Irish forger who is able to take a fifty penny piece and file off the corners so accurately that he can pass it off as a ten penny piece.

RC: And to farm labourer Fred Lurkin who fought for eighteen years to prevent a motorway being built through his kitchen — and won. Now they're building it through his living room.

RB: Then we'll discuss government ministries — are there too many?
We'll be hearing from the Minister of Steak and Kidney Pudding.

RC: But now a message from the police in Finchley. They say that of the two rabbits stolen last week from Peter's Petshop, only fourteen have so far been recovered.

LATER TONIGHT WE'LL BE MEETING...

RB: . . . Mr. Dai Evans, inventor of the Welsh boomerang. It doesn't come back, it *sings* about coming back.

RC: Then we'll meet the Professor from Imperial College with a new theory about what happens when a body is immersed in warm water — the phone rings.

RB: And a Sultan with 365 wives will explain to us why he's looking forward to leap year.

RC: After that we'll be meeting a Tax Inspector who'll show us how to fill in a form, followed by a foreman who'll show us how to fill in a Tax Inspector.

RB: Next we'll interview three French film directors, Jacques Tati, Jacques Scruffi and Jacques Absolutely Falling to Pieces . . .

RC: Then the Romford girl who took the pill washed down with pond water and was today diagnosed as three months stagnant.

RB: Then we'll talk to two inventors, a gunsmith who's invented a sage and onion bullet so you can shoot the goose and stuff it at the same time —

RC: And the insecticide maker who's just produced an aphrodisiac for flies. It doesn't kill them but it lets you swat them two at a time.

RB: Then we'll interview the groundsman who used pansy seed instead of grass seed and queered his pitch.

RC: Maybe we'll have time for a peek at the Cement Marketing Board's Sculpture Exhibition which opened in London today. The main competition was for carvings of the world's great lovers done entirely in limestone. And Casanova won by a long chalk.

RB: And we'll be talking to a generous Scotsman who once every year takes all his money out of the bank for a holiday — and then, when it's had a holiday, he puts it all back again.

RC: Later in our series 'Meet the Workers', we'll talk to an East End docker who has retired after forty years to take a well-earned job.

RB: Then we'll feature the famous colour-blind poet, Mr. Reginald Smithers. Here's an excerpt from one of his lovely poems:

RC: Roses are red,
Violets are brown,
The sky is bright yellow,
And so are bluetits.

RB: And finally we'll be looking at three controversial paintings. Paris seen through the eyes of a Paris artist, Madrid through the eyes of a Madrid artist and Pisa through the eyes of a Pisa artist.

RC: But now a sketch about two workers in a ball bearing factory, in which I play a man who loses his bearings

RB: And I play a man who loses his temper.

And Then We'll Talk To The Man Who Crossed...

RC: . . . A skunk with a Koalo — and got a poo bear.

RB: Then he crossed a truss with a polo mint and got a Nutcracker Suito.

RC: — And a morse code transmitter with a sennapod and got dot dot dot and a very quick dash.

RB: He even crossed a food mixer with a nymphomaniac with a lisp — and got a girl who'll whisk anything.

RC: And a feather with a lady contortionist and got a girl who could tickle her own fancy.

RB: And he actually crossed a table tennis ball with an extremely tall chamber pot and got a ping pong piddle-high poe.

RC: Then we talk to a man who crossed a Gordon Highlander with a moustrap and got a squeaky jockstrap.

RB: And to a scientist from Kuwait who's bred an ostrich with a corkscrew head. You give it a fright and it drills for oil.

RC: And an interior decorator who crossed an elephant with an Axminster rug and got a thick pile on his carpet.

RB: And a very very unlucky man. He crossed an enormous pear tree with a couple of blue tits . . . and got an enormous pair of blue trees . . .

RC: Then we'll talk to a breeder who crossed a dog with a hen and got a poodle that cocks its own doodle.

RB: And a showbiz chef who crossed Raquel Welch with a packet of Bisto and got gravy with very big lumps.

RC: And a chemist who crossed a budgie with a laxative and got a chirrup of figs.

RB: And an Oxford butcher who crossed a turkey with an octopus so the boat crew could have a leg each.

RC: And an expert in animal husbandry who crossed a hen with a banjo and got a chicken that plucks itself.

RB: And a sporting man who crossed a tin of baked beans with two cricket bats and got wind in the willows.

RC: Later on, we'll even meet the ghoul who crossed Dracula with a haystack to create a vampire that sucks you through a straw.

RB: And the man from Colchester who managed to combine a retriever and a tortoise. It goes down to the shops and comes back with last week's paper.

RC: And lastly, a man who's crossed a great dane with a bicycle pump to produce a dog that really puts the wind up postmen.

RB: And his friend, Jack, who crossed a field with Julie Andrews and got nothing at all.

BUT FIRST, THE NEWS

RC: 'This afternoon, Mr. Callaghan left on a tour of friendly countries. He'll be back tomorrow.

RC: President Carter announced today that the U.S. space programme is so short of funds that in future all astronauts who go to the moon will have to pay their own fare.

RB: Meanwhile American astronauts have successfully landed on Mars. Here they encountered a native of the planet, a giant geranium with one huge eye and flippers like a seal. When they approached it the geranium blinked its eye, flipped its flippers, burst into flames and perished. Luckily they managed to take a film of the blinking blooming flipping flaming perishing thing.

RB: His Magnificence the Potentate of Abd el-Wadi returned home tonight after visiting eight other sheikhs in a strenuous round of wife-swapping parties. He now wishes to be known as the Impotentate of Abd el-Wadi.

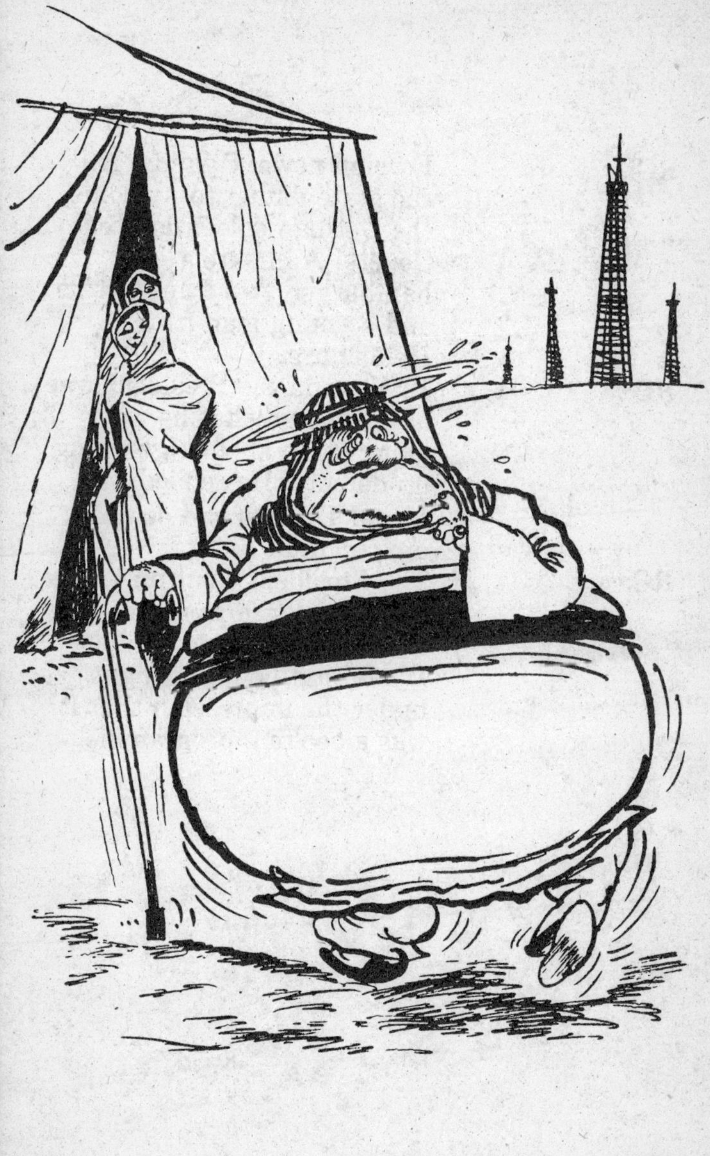

RC: Foreign news. Uganda. At the state dinner to welcome the German delegation today, General Amin ate a hamburger, two frankfurters and a young man from Heidelburg.

RB: In Uganda the President was asked today what he was going to do about tightening up defence. He replied, 'De fence? De man wid de nails am comin to fix it.'

RC: The President went on to say that he wished to return the twenty-six episodes of Pot Black that he had bought under the impression that it was a cooking programme.

WE INTERRUPT THE NEWS FOR A POLICE MESSAGE...

RB: ... here is a police message for Mr. and Mrs. Smith, believed to be spending the weekend in Brighton. Will Mr. Smith please return to his home in Chorley where his wife, Mrs. Jackson, is absolutely furious.

RC: British customs officials have arrested a famous Russian woman spy after the discovery of two miniature radios hidden in the cups of her bra. Said an official, 'We became suspicious when from the top of her dress we heard Kenneth McKellar singing, "The Hills are Alive with the Sound of Music".'

RB: A Danish importer who lost a trunkful of highly pornographic books on the luggage escalator at London Airport has at last managed to find them. His trunk came up last Wednesday — and his case comes up next Thursday.

RC: But the recent airline strike has meant that a Hampshire woman not only had to carry her luggage onto the plane but also had to finish her journey by rail. She claimed she left Hurn by plane for Albania and arrived at Albania by train with a hernia.

RB: A beautiful young Swedish girl who'd gone swimming in the nude was rescued today by the crew of a Scottish trawler. To save her embarrassment they quickly covered her with an old macintosh — Mr. Angus Macintosh of Fyfe — who was delighted.

RB: British scientists too made history this week in the field of interbreeding when they crossed a skunk with a fairy and got a whiffenpouf.

RB: And now a sketch featuring Mr. Ronnie Corbett who this year made a lot of money on the greyhounds — as a jockey.

NEWS
AROUND BRITAIN

RC: British Rail announced today that the price of coffee is to go up to 20p a slice.

RB: But first, here is some good news. The pound had another good day yesterday. It rose sharply at ten o'clock then had a light breakfast and went for a stroll in the park.

RC: This contrasts with last week when the pound closed at only 2.4 against the Matabele Gumbo Bead.

RB: A survey on the decline of morals in Britain reveals that in Liverpool alone on each day last week an average of 267 women made love to an unmarried man. The man is now recovering in hospital.

RC: Mr. Osbert Grove, Britain's worst ever postman, who claims he was wrongfully dismissed by the GPO, today delivered a petition to the Queen — at 15 Station Street, Scunthorpe.

RB: In a new drive to improve the standards of service and hygiene a West End hotel today dismissed a waiter for having his thumb in the soup . . . They also dismissed a topless waitress for two similar offences.

RC: The Family Planning Association announced that in Britain 90% of all parents are, or have been, on the pill. And 85% of them are women.

RB: Of these 85%, 20% are now on it and 13% are now off it, 12% are on it on and off and 9% are off it off and on, 8% are often on it, 7% are often off it, 6% are off it and wish they were on it and 4% are on it and off it so seldom it doesn't matter. 3% are don't knows, 2% are don't cares, 1% are no, don'ts and Mrs. Ivy Whizzer was disqualified for ruining her entrance form.

RC: There was a record number of births in Kilburn this week. Apparently it was all due to the Irish Sweep. But he's now moved to Camden Town.

RB: From the world of nature in the raw comes first the news that a female streaker disturbed patrons at the Albert Hall today. Luckily she was caught by the bouncers and ejected.

RC: And it appears that in Hexham this evening a mad dog bit an income tax inspector. After being given injections and treatment for shock the dog has been allowed to go home.

RB: It was explained tonight why Shepherds Bush town hall are flying the Royal standard at half mast — they're half expecting the Queen.

RC:	Short sighted Lady Myopia Fotheringay was in the news again when she opened the new haberdashery centre at Slough by cutting a ceremonial ribbon. As she did so, a large crowd cheered and her knickers fell down.

RB: It's announced in Newport Pagnell this evening that Mr. Horace Whipsley, the world's most superstitious motorist, known for the lucky horseshoe dangling in his rear window, the sprig of heather on his wipers, the St. Christopher suspended from his dashboard and the four rabbit's feet in his glove compartment — was run over by thirteen steamrollers.

RC: Speaking today at the Weymouth W.I., an unmarried mother of three blamed her situation on the fact that she was sheltered too much when younger. First in a bus shelter, then in an old air-raid shelter, then a taxi shelter . . . . .

RB: And finally, millionaire Jock McScrooge opens his new cinema in Peebles today, known as 'The Peebles Theatre', with a special offer. Old age pensioners are admitted free — if accompanied by their parents.

RC: But now a sketch featuring Mr. Ronnie Barker who only today was presented with an illuminated address by his neighbours — they set his house on fire.

NEWS FROM THE IRISH

RB: In Dublin, the convention of Irish wizards announce today that due to wet weather, the rain-making ceremony will not be held in Phoenix Park. Instead, it will be held in City Hall.

RC: And it was also announced in Dublin that the Irish Doomsday Book is in fact a forgery. This was the conclusion after a six-month study of it by typewriting experts.

RB: But here is good news. The Irish Guinness shortage was solved today. From tomorrow, customers will be served with lager and sunglasses.

RC: And Mr. Patrick O'Flynn of Dublin was arrested for streaking through a nudist camp.

RB: Police broke into the home of Ireland's most brilliant forger today and took away two million seven-pound notes.

RC: When a clever gang of thieves were caught red handed in a Dublin bank police immediately sealed all the exits — so the gang escaped through all the entrances.

RB: There was a disturbance at Hampton Court Maze this afternoon. A party of Irish trippers panicked when they couldn't find their way in.

RC: The Irish Times published its £20,000 prize competition crossword today. For those who don't wish to take part, the answers are on page nine.

RB: And later tonight we'll have a commentary on the launching of the Irish Moon Rocket — if they can find a bottle big enough to take the stick.

RC: But now a sketch about ghosts and ghouls in which I get caught by the ghosties —

RB: — And I get caught by surprise.

NEWS FROM THE SCOTS

RC: In London's West End tonight a Scotsman collapsed from starvation after spending five weeks on the back seat of a pay-as-you-leave bus.

RB: And Home Office researchers have at last determined what Scotsmen do with old razor blades. They shave with them.

WELCH NEWS

RC: The goodwill tour of British sporting fixtures by Miss Racquel Welch has been causing certain embarrassments this week. At St. Andrews Miss Welch has had a hole in one . . . and a very interesting split in the other.

RB: But now a sketch starring Mr. Ronnie Corbett who in fact buys all his suits off the peg — at any shop selling Action Man.

A WORD ABOUT TONIGHT'S ENTERTAINMENT

RC: Well, first of all, Duncan McHoot, the well-known Scots drunkard, will play Amazing Grace on the breathalyser.

RB: Then we'll see another Scot, Jock McClog, a one-legged kilt dancer from the Gorbals, who specialises in high kicks and falling over.

RC: The Tooting Unmarried Mothers' Operatic Society will be singing Get me to the Church on Time.

RB: They'll be accompanied by the Massed Mounted Bands of the Household Cavalry closely followed by the Massed Buckets of the Rhubarb Growers' Association.

RC: And as light relief, veteran fan dancer Mimi La Zouche will perform The Dance of the Virgin entirely from memory.

RB: After this, Antonio, the famous Spanish dancer, will dance the fandango — with his fan in one hand and his dango in the other.

RC: Then we'll have another celebrated Scottish musician. We'll be privileged to hear the oldest bagpiper in Scotland, Mr. Jock McDougal, who in World War One played so well in battle that the enemy used to shout out requests.

RB: This will be followed by a demonstration of sixteen ways of cooking sennapods by the Galloping Gourmet.

RC: And we're proud to feature the world's most short-sighted knife-thrower, Rudolpho Colenzo the Second and his assistant, Zelda the Twenty-ninth.

RB: Then we'll look at some unusual dances including the Gay Gordons, The Nice Nigels and the Queer Quistophers.

RC: As a finale a very lovely young physical education mistress will do a novelty dance covered only in blackboard chalk — but the novelty soon wears off.

RB: We'll end with two rather unusual items. We'll have with us Mr. Dudley Wilford who yesterday on his hundredth birthday was arrested for chasing 23 young women at an athletics meeting. He received a summons from the court and a telegram of congratulation from the Queen.

RC: And the climax will be the unveiling of the very latest brassiere. It's called The Sheepdog — it rounds them up and points them in the right direction.

RB: But now a sketch set in Frankenstein's castle in which I take the very important part of the monster

RC: And I make him put it back.

AND NOW THE MAIN NEWS. POLITICS.

RB: The Prime Minister held a meeting with the Cabinet today. He also spoke to the bookcase and argued with the chest of drawers.

RC: But tomorrow the Prime Minister will receive a secret visit from Mr. Brezhnev, according to informed sources in Moscow. Completely *un*informed sources stated: 'We don't know anything about it.'

RB: The Chancellor has announced new plans for shortening the dole queues. He's asking the men to stand closer together.

RC: However, in a white paper today the Government revealed plans for the small shopkeeper — a lower counter.

RB: And the Prime Minister announced today a new plan to ensure that we don't all suddenly become poor when we reach sixty — he's going to make sure we're all poor when we reach thirty.

RC: Later, at Downing Street, the Premier was met by a delegation of squatters — but they wouldn't let him in.

RB: There was an embarrassing incident at Madame Tussaud's last week when Mr. Denis Healey unveiled the wax model of himself and his chauffeur drove it back to Westminster by mistake. Luckily it had only attended three cabinet meetings before it was discovered.

IN THE HOUSE OF COMMONS LAST NIGHT...

RC: ... when the heating failed, MPs had to don spare overalls to keep warm. Mr. Callaghan wore four pairs whilst Mrs. Thatcher wore three pairs, an overall majority of one.

RB: Mrs. Thatcher went on to remind the House that before long this country would have a woman Prime Minister. Mr. Edward Heath said, 'I heartily agree.' Mr. Heath was wearing a powder blue dress with matching hat and accessories.

RC: And a secret diary just published reveals what MPs ate for their Christmas dinners last year. It seems Mr. Callaghan had the usual turkey — while Mrs. Thatcher bought a new one.

RB: After an all-night sitting in the House of Commons all parties have now agreed it must have been the curry.

RC: In one dramatic incident last night, Mr. Cyril Smith rose from the Liberal Front Bench — and the rest of the party fell off the other end.

RB: At the end of a heated session tempers cooled in the Commons bar. Mr. Callaghan bought Mrs. Thatcher a pink gin, she bought Mr. Powell a black gin and he bought Mr. Wedgwood-Benn a pint of Evostick.

BUT THERE'S BAD NEWS FROM...

RC: . . . Manchester, where a teacher with special responsibility for sex education at a comprehensive school today eloped with one of his visual aids.

THOUGH THERE'S GOOD NEWS FROM...

RB: . . . the North Atlantic. After years of expensive and dangerous work at the site of the Titanic sinking, Irish salvage experts today raised the iceberg.

RC: And a ninety-two-year-old Wigtown man was married today to an eighteen-year-old girl. At the reception afterwards, her friends gave her a long woolly comforter and his friends gave him about two months.

RB: In the sketch that follows, I shall be practising for the Eisteddfod.

RC: And I shall be practising for the Lowsteddfod.

LATER ON THIS EVENING WE'LL BE TALKING TO...

RB: . . . Mr. Herbert Gudge who has tattooed the whole of his body with old masters. He has a Botticelli on his chest, a Constable under each arm, a Watteau down the back, a Whistler up the front — and the inscrutable smile of the Mona Lisa becomes a broad grin whenever he sits down . . .

RC: And a fifty-year-old doctor who claims that smoking takes years off your life. He says that if he hadn't smoked when he was younger he'd now be 63.

RB: And the Irishman who plans to cross the Atlantic on a plank when he can find one that's long enough.

RC: And even the clumsy owner of a fish and chip shop with a long record of wife-battering.

RB: Then I'll be having a word with the song and dance man who yesterday put on a happy face, buttoned up his overcoat, pulled on his fancy pants and zippered his doodah.

RC: And we'll be introducing two young women of leisure who last week took hours off in their garden. And looking forward to the time when they take theirs off in our garden.

RB: Then we go on to interview three Indian princes, the Mufti of Baroda, the Lounge Suit of Hyberabad and the Bedsock of Bangalore.

RC: And we'll have a talk on Ethics — by a man from Thuthex.

RB: Attractive Olga Follanova will discuss the sex lives of three great Russians, Boris Godanov, Boris Not-Quite-Godanov, and Boris Absolutely-Useless.

RC: Then in our series, Great Optimists of Our Time, we'll visit the Royal Hospital for Chelsea Pensioners and talk to the man who designed the maternity wing.

RB: After this we'll have three contrasting pieces of choral music; sacred songs from St. Martin-in-the-Fields, rather less sacred songs from St. Christopher-in-the-Woods, and some positively revolting songs from St. Vitus-in-the-Long-Grass-Behind-the-Glue-Factory.

RC: We'll show you the new Mafia scarecrow. It's so terrifying, not only do the birds not take any seeds, they bring back the seeds they took last year.

RB: And, by the way, later in the programme, Monsieur Pierre Bouffon, France's most amorous football manager, will tell us of his club's progress in the European Cup, and why he's always glad to get the first leg over.

RC: And we'll have with us a man who is so superstitious he got stuck in a lift with thirteen strippers and pressed the alarm button.

RB: Finally we'll be looking at the works of three distinguished poets — Gerard Manley Hopkins, Gerard Not-So-Manly Hopkins and Gerard Out-And-Out Raving Fairy Hopkins.

RC: But now a sketch featuring Mr. Ronnie Barker as a nudist who can't add up, and has to count on his friends.

BRITISH SCIENTISTS DO IT AGAIN...

RB: . . . Which puts them in second place behind French scientists who do it again and again.

RC: Government agricultural experts announce a revolutionary new insecticide. It kills all the crops so the insects starve to death.

RB: And important statistics are revealed today about why husbands get out of bed at night. It seems 5% get up with insomnia, 10% get up to go to the bathroom and 85% get up and go home.

RC: The research team went on to investigate the social habits of 'Mr. and Mrs. Average'. But unfortunately Mr. Average was not at home. He'd slipped down to Brighton with Mrs. Well-Above-Average.

RB: We interrupt this bulletin for a police message. Will the man who lost eight bottles of whisky at Euston station this morning please go to the Lost Property office by Platform Nine where the man who found them has just been handed in.

EXPLORATION

RC:	And there's news today of a South American tribe where the women make themselves attractive by covering their skins in mud, rotting brussel sprouts and linseed oil. The tribe is extinct.
RB:	Sir Hartley Withers, the explorer, has had a fantastic escape. He was being pursued along a river bank by three hungry lions, and just as it seemed they were certain to catch him, he was eaten by a crocodile.

AND NEWS FROM THE ZOOS

RC: We've just heard sensational news from Whipsnade. The male panda, who's developed a passion for music, has mated with the Head Keeper's harmonium. Experts say this may create a pandamonium.

RB: But the giant worm failed to mate at London Zoo again today. Its rear end had a headache.

RC: At Chessington Zoo last night, Mr. and Mrs. Horace Bungstrom were accidentally locked in an empty cage at closing time. This is the first time that Mr. and Mrs. Bungstrom have mated in captivity.

RB: Whilst the Zoological Society have just issued a new report on the mating of animals. Apparently ostriches mate once a week, crocodiles three times a week and elephants three weeks a time.

ARCHAEOLOGISTS NOW SAY...

RC: . . . That they know who the first spectators ever to invade the playing area were. It was a party of Irishmen who ran onto the pitch at the Coliseum to get the lions' autographs.

RB: The teeth of a prehistoric mammoth were found today in Sussex. This is a double event, according to the man who found them, Professor Alan Turpie. Not only are they the world's oldest tooth but they were found in the world's largest glass of water.

RC: And now here's tomorrow's weather forecast: the sun will be killing 'em in Gillingham, it'll be choking in Woking, dry in Rye and cool in Goole. And if you live in Lissingdown take an umbrella.

RB: And what's more, it's going to be seventy degrees — twenty in the morning, thirty at midday and twenty in the evening.

►

MEDICINE

RC: The National Health Service state today they're getting so behindhand that for the Pregnancy Testing Service there is now a ten month waiting list.

RB: But at Golders Green Maternity Hospital the wife of a well known ventriloquist has just given birth to a nine pound gouncing gagy goy.

RC: And a spokesman from Warbleton Cottage Hospital said today there was no need to operate on the man who swallowed half a scrabble set. He said the problem will eventually solve itself though not in so many words.

RB: Whilst a man who swallowed a barometer was admitted to Cheadle Cottage Hospital tonight. His condition was described as 'Set fair — stormy later'.

RC: A young woman from Wealdstone made an extremely serious complaint today against a famous cosmetic surgeon. She said he gave her a perfect bust but made it far too big. Having weighed the evidence, the Police have put it in the hands of the Public Prosecutor.

RB: And we've just heard that National Health doctors have staged a protest march down Harley Street waving big placards written out by themselves. Unfortunately no one could read the placards except one chemist who was passing. He told them to come back in ten minutes.

RC: In another complaint against the Health Service a patient said he was rushed around the country for a series of emergency operations. He had a hand operation at Neasden and a knee operation at Handsworth. Then he had a heart transplant at Liverpool and a liver transplant at Hartlepool.

RB: — Then he had a hair transplant at Littlehampton and on arriving at Harefield he fainted.

RC: Reports that British doctors are trying to specialise in too many branches of medicine were denied today by Doctor Cedric Milford, an ear, nose, throat, dandruff and belly button consultant.

RB: Britain's first pregnant man complained tonight about his treatment by the Press. He said, 'All this publicity makes me sick — especially in the mornings.'

RC: It's reported that two eminent doctors who examined the ears of one of Britain's leading politicians are concerned about what they saw. They saw each other.

RB: British Rail research scientists have come up with a new serum for the common cold. It doesn't cure the cold but your nose will only run in good weather.

RC: Finally there's good news for deaf people. The Sex Pistols issued another LP today.

RB: We must now break off for an important police message: You're warned to be on the look out for Joseph Gomez, a Spaniard, last heard of living in Tooting, whose mother was in a convent on the Costa Brava. A one-time flautist with a symphony orchestra, he is wanted for looting in Haifa, where he worked on a farm. The police urge people to look out for a Haifa Looting Fluting Tooting Son of a Nun from Barcelona, Part-Time Ploughboy Joe.

BUSINESS NEWS– A MERGER IS ANNOUNCED…

RC: . . . Between B.A.C. and Cyril Lords — to make flying carpets for the Persian market.

RB: And Pye records have merged with Apple records to make Apple Pyes.

RC: — The Noise Abatement Society and the Kennel Club have joined forces to produce Hush Puppies.

RB: — And Krispie Bacon Limited have merged with Rolls Royce to make Sausage Rolls and Royce Krispies.

RC: We've also heard that Achilles Cleaning Powder have joined up with Scottish Distilleries to produce a cleaner that kills 99% of all known germs — and makes the other 1% too drunk to bother.

RB: And Mothercare are joining British Leyland to produce a car with a built-in rattle.

INDUSTRIAL RELATIONS

RC: Better news today from the National Coal Board. They say there was no absenteeism in British pits last month. All the absentees stayed at home.

RB: Figures released today show that two out of every ten men work for a nationalised industry. While the other eight sit and watch them.

RC: But a retiring Liverpool docker aged 65 stated that he'd never had a day's illness in his life — he always made it last a week.

RB: Girl strippers in Old Compton Street who've been on strike accepted a motion to return to work, after a show of hands — knees and bumpsidaisy.

RC: While at a Birmingham factory this afternoon a man lost two fingers in an accident. He didn't actually notice the loss until he was saying goodnight to the foreman.

RB: Another factory in Birmingham laid off 500 car body workers. They said, 'We can't find work for them. We only make digestive biscuits.'

AND BRITISH RAIL ANNOUNCE...

RC: . . . That they have developed a new engine so fast that it can travel from London to Reading before its driver gets a pay rise.

RB: And some happy news from British Rail. Agatha Wainwright, the station announcer at Victoria, today married engine driver Dick Crankshawe. Her dress was of white organdie with lace bodice and her train was twenty minutes late.

RC: But there was chaos at King's Cross today when a consignment of ninety-three tortoises from Indonesia escaped from a guard's van and made off along the platform. When asked how the tortoises managed to get clean away the Stationmaster said, 'We tried to stop them but they were just too fast for our porters.'

RB: In the sketch that follows, which has been carefully cast by our new Irish producer, I play the part of Ronnie Corbett . . .

NEWS From British Leyland?

RC: It was announced in London today that British Leyland have given up the old clocking-on system. Workers will now be invited to sign the Visitor's Book.

RB: Two Exeter newly-weds who won a competition that offered a honeymoon 'away from it all' in guaranteed quiet and seclusion are grateful to British Leyland who've booked them into the back seat of a Rover on the production line.

RC: And we've just heard that British Leyland strikers have been fitting silencers to the motor horns — and now the cars don't give a hoot either.

RB: But now a sketch featuring Mr. Ronnie Corbett, whose wife thinks he's the salt of the earth. That's why she keeps him in the cellar.

LATER WE'LL DISCUSS THE BURNING QUESTIONS...

RC: ... What should you tip the porter in an all-male nudist camp — and will a pound note cover it?

RB: Prince Rainier of Monaco — has he fallen from Grace?

RC: Education — can cross eyed teachers control their pupils?

RB: Pilfering coalminers — do they have lots of slack in their trousers?

RC: And British deep sea divers with chicken pox — do they come up to scratch?

RB: Then we'll be discussing potholing and why it ruins your bedroom carpets.

RC: And a very wealthy man who was a snow plough driver in Trinidad will tell us how he fiddled his overtime.

RB: And in our new series 'Medical Hints by Well Known Actresses' tonight your very own Googie Withers — and what to do if it does.

RC: Later a well known patriotic gambler will tell us why he's backing Britain — he's getting two thousand to one against.

RB: Then we'll consider loneliness, with a special report from the Archbishop of Golders Green.

RC: And a famous millionaire will reveal how it feels to have piles of gold . . . wealthy but uncomfortable.

RB: Then we'll discuss the bread shortage with a man who's been throwing IOUs to the ducks.

RC: And for ladies we'll be talking about rum babas — and what to wear if you've got them.

RB: We'll be discussing four new Classic series — 'What Katy Did', 'What Katy Did Next', 'Who Did What to Katy' and 'Son of Katy'.

RC: Which will lead us to discuss three famous oriental sex books, the Kama Sutra, the Less Calm Sutra and the Absolutely Frantic Sutra.

At This Point We Had Hoped To...

RB: . . . Present the dance group, The Five Foolish Virgins, but we've found out that two of them are really quite clever —

RC: And the other three are down with flu.

RB: And we're sorry to say that after further objections about West Indian bouncers, we've cancelled tonight's demonstration by the Trinidad Ladies Go-Go Dancers.

RC: At this point we had also hoped to interview the world's oldest man, but unfortunately he's had to cry off due to the unexpected illness of his father . . .

RB: So we were to have had Jimmy Savile with us but we've just heard that his suit has been disallowed by the Noise Abatement Society.

RC: But now a sketch featuring Mr. Ronnie Barker, a man who's so modest that whcn he recently published his autobiography he wasn't even mentioned in it.

Society Gossip

RB: Complaints were made following the Chef's Annual Fancy Dress Ball last night. It seems a woman dressed only in gooseberries and cream made improper suggestions to a man dressed in cake and sherry. She made a proper fool of herself and got a trifle excited.

RC: The Annual General Meeting of the Claustrophobia Society at the Albert Hall was a fiasco. Only one member turned up and he kept shouting, 'Let me out!'

RB: And the President of the Sex Change Association, Mr Daphne Smith, is to marry Miss George Watson. Miss Watson, the former Mr Angela Watson will marry Mr Smith, the former Miss Henry Smith, at St John's Wood Registry Office, the former St Martha's Wood Registry Office.

RC: In the National Dance Festival at Finsbury this evening the crowd became so excited police had to link arms and hold them back. They were pushed forward four times but each time they struggled back again. The police were commended for their restraint and awarded first prize in the hokey cokey.

RB: Whilst at the annual meeting of the Squatters' Association, the Minister of Housing gave his usual address. And fifteen members moved into it.

RC: Fanny Cradock has announced that she's to join Women's Lib. When asked if she would be burning her bra she said, 'No darling, I'll sautée it with onions and a little white wine'.

RB: And, indeed, the President of the Winetasters' Association today paid tribute to their retiring secretary, Mrs. Prudence Vine. He described her as 'plucky and full bodied and well worth laying down for a couple of years'.

RC: Good news from the West Ham Short-Sighted Society. They held a picnic on Clapham Common . . . And the East Ham Short-Sighted Society held a picnic on the West Ham Short-Sighted Society.

RB: There's less good news from the National Conference of Henpecked Husbands at the South Norwood Astrodrome. The conference failed to turn up. It had to go and mow the lawn.

RC: And a Watford man has made a serious complaint against the Sunnyview Naturists' Paradise. He said that after being in the nudist camp for at least three months he had a letter from the secretary that began, 'Dear Sir or Madam . . .'.

RB: Another disappointed guest at Sunnyview was a member of the Charles Dickens Society's annual nudist weekend. He had Great Expectations but it was a very Bleak House and everybody laughed at his Little Dorritt.

RC: A man who threw his mother-in-law into the crocodile pool at Belleview Zoo has been prosecuted by the RSPCA.

RB: And a Hull man has also been prosecuted for cruelty by the RSPCA. He bought a homing pigeon and moved house.

RC: And we end with an important message from the Royal Society for the Prevention of Accidents. Since most accidents happen in your home — they advise you to move.

Social Diary

RB: At the big Fancy Dress Ball last night given by the Football Pools Federation, a young lady arrived entirely naked except for a cross marked on each bosom. She was allowed in when she explained that she was a chest of draws.

RC: The Art World. The engagement was announced today between the famous post impressionist Madeleine Renoir and Mr. Percy Edwards, the famous animal impersonator. They met when he was giving his impression of a dog and she was giving her impression of a post.

COURT CIRCULAR

RB: Following the dispute with the Domestic Servants Union at Buckingham Palace today, the Queen, a radiant figure in white silk gown and crimson robe, swept down the main staircase and through the hall — then she dusted the cloakroom and hoovered the lounge.

RC: And in the show jumping at the Badminton Horse Trials, Princess Anne once again left her mark. So he had to go home by bus.

RB: We've just heard that Her Majesty the Queen went on a short informal walkabout today after she hit her thumb with a hammer.

BUS STOP

Meanwhile, Reports Are Coming In...

RC: . . . Of a freak tidal wave in Birmingham, mountain avalanches in Norfolk, six-foot snowdrifts in the North Sea and a very good party at the Met Office.

RB: And news has just come in from Magalumbu, the primitive Pacific island where a man has been condemned to death for cannibalism. This morning, the day of his execution, the condemned man rose, got dressed, cleaned his teeth and ate a hearty warder.

RC: In the next sketch I play the all conquering warlord Genghis Khan.

RB: And I play his unhappy brother, Genghis Khant.

NEWS OF SHOW BUSINESS

RC: The record company who recently released Rod McKuen's Greatest Hits without a hole in the middle today offered the following advice to buyers. Take a Polo mint and, using it as a template, bore a hole through the centre of the record. For even better results, play the Polo mint.

RB: Mick Jagger was overwhelmed by fans at Los Angeles Airport this morning. The police linked arms to give him mouth-to-mouth resuscitation.

RC: And we've just heard that Racquel Welch has been signed to play Quasimodo in a new film entitled 'The Hunchfront of Notre Dame'.

RB: We've also heard that due to the electricians' strike 'Oh Calcutta!' is to be renamed 'Fanny by Gaslight'.

RC: When floodwater filled the Festival Hall last night, the seventeen stone contralto, Renata Lindstrom, escaped by floating through the doors on a double bass. She was accompanied by Donald Swann on the piano.

RB: And we've just heard that 'Amazing Grace' has gone to number eight with Gladys Knight and The Pips at number nine. Mr. Callaghan at number ten said 'It's ruining the tone of the neighbourhood.'

RC: Last night at the Excelsior Ballroom, Kilburn, the Shamrock Showband did request time. When asked to do something Irish, they dug up the car park.

RB: Shirley Bassey has just has a single come out. . . one of the straps broke on her dress.

RC: And due to heavy fog in Central London, Susan Hampshire, who's playing Peter Pan, couldn't land at the Coliseum and had to be diverted to Manchester Opera House.

RB: From Hollywood Zsa Zsa Gabor has announced that owing to illness she has cancelled all her engagements for three months — but her marriages will go ahead as planned.

RC: And lastly, Turville Dinge, the celebrated budgerigar impressionist died today. A few friends attended a private ceremony at which he was flushed down the lavatory.

THERE WAS A CRISIS IN A CIRCUS...

RB: ... At Bletchley today when the lion escaped and threw the whole place into a panic. The strongest man in the world fainted and the indiarubber man completely erased the tattooed lady.

RC: And at Lord George Davidson's Circus it was a disastrous day for the Yallop Brothers. First, Arthur Yallop, the human ostrich, got his head stuck in the sand . . .

RB: Then Billy Yallop, the human cannonball, was fired . . .

RC: And lastly, Charlie Yallop, the human fly, committed insecticide.

RB: We also hear that in support of their salary claim, the Irish Wall of Death Riders' Association starts a go-slow today.

RC: In the next sketch I play the hero who bravely saves a sweet young girl from molestation — by taking a cold shower.

COMPETITION ROUND-UP

RB: Four girls were disqualified for cheating in the Miss Greater Manchester competition last night. They were Miss Altrincham, Miss Paddingham, Miss Pumpingham and Miss Stuffingham.

JUDGE
MISS PUMPINGHAM 78

RC: Whilst in the World Plumbing Championships in Oslo, the Dutch entry was flooded, the Icelandic entry froze, the Chinese entry was disqualified for flushing from right to left and the British entry said it would be round first thing in the morning.

RB: In Belper, this evening, Mr. Dudley Arkwright ate 622 radishes in six minutes twenty-three seconds. This doesn't count as a world record as he had a following wind.

RC: At the Do-It-Yourself furniture competition at Olympia the favourite was Mrs. Cynthia Bollinger with her mahogany desk. But we've now heard she was disqualified at the last minute. Her legs were too bowed and when the Judge banged her bottom her drawers fell off.

AND THE WINNERS...

RB: The annual London 'Health and Beauty' contest was won today by Miss Wapping. Second was Miss Not-Quite-So-Wapping, and third was Miss Absolutely-Piffling.

RC: Agriculture. Mr. Ernest Waldron, a cattle expert who's spent his whole life examining the back legs of cows, was given a special award today. Said Mr. Waldron, 'This is not the first time I've had a pat on the back.'

RB: The title of the most considerate father of the year goes to Mr. Clarence Larkin of Stroud. He put a silencer on his shotgun because his daughter wanted a quiet wedding.

RC: The Harrow School garlic-eating contest has been won by the same boy for the third year running. His headmaster said today. 'This definitely puts him in a class by himself.'

RB: Mr. Ernest Quigley, the winner of the sponsored hairdressing marathon who's had his hair permed and set nonstop for 73 hours was today described as completely and utterly lacquered.

RC: And George Mumble, the Bodmin man who swallowed two hundredweight of cascara for a bet on Coronation Night, today celebrated his Silver Jubilee. He's been on the throne for twenty-five years.

RB: And now a sketch about enormous embarrassments at a small intimate party. Ronnie Corbett will play the small intimate party and I will play the enormous embarrassments.

THIS WEEK'S AWARDS

RC: Mr. Nigel Whipster, a window dresser for thirty years, today received the Queen's Award for Industry — and his flat mate, Rupert, received the Industry's Award for Queens.

RB: The man who invented the zip fastener was today honoured with a life peerage. He'll now be known as the Lord of the Flies.

RC: Tremendous results have been achieved by a team of British scientists who made ten laboratory rats smoke twenty cigarettes a day for a whole year. For this the team has been awarded the Nobel Prize — and the rats have got a colour telly with the coupons.

RB: Today's anniversaries: Jimmy Tarbuck had a telegram from the Queen today. His jokes were exactly one hundred years old.

RC: And shy spinster, Hester Pettigrew, was awarded the George Cross for saving the life of a drowning man. She gave him the kiss of life with her bicycle pump.

RB: Finally, it was announced tonight that the Husband of the Year has accepted the Nurse of the Year's Offer of the Month. They've gone off for the Dirty Weekend of the Century.

BUT HERE'S A SPECIAL ANNOUNCEMENT...

RC: The Government is to levy V.A.T. on words. This means that a lot of words will have to be shorter. Now here's tomorrow's news:
The Quee and the Duk of Ed flew by Conc last nig to visit Mr. Cart. Meanwhile at Cow in the Is of Wig, Mr. Ed Heat won the Cow yac race in his bra new yac. Lat footba res: Tott Hot two, Arse nil.

RB: We've been asked by the Health Service to explain the use of the hospital bell. In fact you should ring it once if you need anything, twice if it's urgent and three times if it's too late.

RC: And we've advice for the ladies. If your electric blanket doesn't work, switch it off at once and call in a man.

RB: Now here is a special announcement. Police report exceptionally heavy traffic over Putney Bridge. It's been so heavy in fact that one woman had to abandon her car and continue her driving test on foot.

RC: Good news for Peeping Toms. The lady who runs the famous Aunt Maud advice column has agreed to help them . . . she's going to leave her bedroom curtains open on Thursdays.

RB: And British Rail announce a new service for naughty couples going to Brighton — the have-it-away-day.

RC: The Gay Lib recruiting vehicle may be touring your area this week. It's easy to recognize. It's mauve in colour and the number plate is RU 1-2.

RB: We've just been handed an urgent warning about Trimmet's Treacle Puddings, which have caused several people to be sent to hospital with badly scalded feet. It seems people have misunderstood the instructions which read, 'Before opening tin, stand in boiling water for twenty minutes.'

TRIMM
TREAC
PUDDI

RC: We must apologise for a fault in today's farming programme, 'Compost for Beginners'. Vision and sound have failed. The programme will continue in smell only.

RB: But here is an important message for long wave listeners: you can stop waving now.

RC: Lastly we have to apologize for an earlier bulletin concerning a prisoner who escaped from a South African gaol. We should have said he was a trusty prisoner who escaped in The Rand — not a randy prisoner who escaped in a truss.

ADVICE SECTION

RB: The B.M.A. has asked us to give a simple piece of advice to men who wish to avoid falling hair. Get out of the way.

RC: After our beauty advice last week a young lady has written to us about her worried frown and overdeveloped bust — but we advise her to grin and bear it.

MESSAGES

RB: Here is a message for seven honeymoon couples in a hotel in Peebles: breakfast was served three days ago.

RC: Arnold Crump, a six foot nine, ham-fisted hairy drunk with a short temper, bad breath, acne, dandruff and fleas was named by Scotland Yard today as Britain's most Unwanted Man.

INCIDENTS & ACCIDENTS

RB: There was an incident in a Walsall topless bar tonight when a member of the Campaign for Real Ale said the beer was all right, but his waitress was flat.

RC: And there was an unhappy moment at Kings Cross station tonight when a Scottish football fan lost all his luggage moments after stepping off the train. The cork came out.

RB: A row has developed over Sussex County Council's new library catalogue for 1978. It lists the B.R. timetable under fiction.

RC: And Temperance Toyshops are to withdraw a thousand-piece nude jigsaw of Tom Jones unless seventy-three pieces are withdrawn.

RB: In the English Channel a ship carrying red paint has collided with a ship carrying purple paint. It is believed that both crews have been marooned.

RC: Sir Hartley Fawcett, crackshot big game hunter, famous for his slogan 'Shoot 'em right between the eyes!', was eaten late last night by two one-eyed tigers walking arm in arm.

RB: And there was an accident involving Britain's worst goalkeeper, Bill Berkley, who has already let through 157 goals this season. Shouting out 'I am a complete failure,' Berkley threw himself in front of a bus . . . luckily the bus passed under him and he wasn't hurt.

RC: There was a nasty accident at a Hollywood Bowling Alley today when Telly Savalas bent to do up a shoelace. A passer-by stuck two fingers up his nostrils.

RB: But Sir Wilbury Chintz, the famous upholstery expert who yesterday fell into a fabric loom, is said to be almost completely recovered.

RC: Now a sketch in which Mr. Ronnie Barker plays the part of a bridegroom who finds there is no bed in the honeymoon suite and has to stand up for his conjugal rights.

CRIME

RB: From the world of crime we've just heard that the series of thefts from cabinet ministers still goes on. Tonight we talk to the Minister without Portfolio, the Minister without a Bicycle and the Minister without Trousers.

RC: A man who was caught peeking into the changing cubicles at an outsize women's dress shop described himself as a quantity surveyor.

RB: And at a certain church in Hertfordshire both the Vicar and his housekeeper have been suspended. They found his vest in her pantry and her pants in his vestry.

POLICE FIFTEEN

RC: 8000 cases of imported fruit were stolen from Liverpool docks today. A police spokesman said, 'It would have taken a gang of dock thieves at least four hours to do this.' A spokesman for the dockers said, 'What happens in the tea break is none of our concern.'

RB: Mr. Lemuel Shift, described as the world's sneakiest little man, denied today that he'd been to Scotland Yard to take a lie detector test. If there was one missing, he said, it was nothing to do with him.

RC: In another incident, West Kensington Police questioned a man with a wooden leg who was hopping down the High Street while pouring a tin of treacle over his bald head. The man explained that he was going to a fancy dress ball as a toffee apple.

RB: But it seems the perfect crime was committed last night when thieves broke into Scotland Yard itself and stole all the toilets. Police say they haven't a single thing to go on.

POLICE MEASURES

RB: The grave of Sir Cheevely Robley, the jam tycoon, was opened by police today. On the lid of the coffin they found the words. 'To open, pierce with a pin and prise lid off with a penny.'

RC: Streakers in the Greater London area are now being faced with Scotland Yard's latest counter-measure; police dogs with wet noses.

RB: A pickpocket who was chased out of Battersea Funfair took refuge today in the Post Office Tower. Police immediately threw a ring round it — and the Postmaster General gave them a goldfish.

RC: 'Police are clamping down on dealers who make fortunes selling stolen cars which have been sawn in half and welded to other vehicles,' said Superintendent Hackett from the wheel of his E type combine harvester today.

A MAN WAS DETAINED...

RC: ... At Saville Row Police Station today after an incident involving a topless model in an Oxford Street store window. He was later arrested and charged with a smash and two grabs.

RB: Two Irishmen were apprehended when they broke into a Dublin bookmakers and lost £800. The two men charged were Terence Finnegan who gave his address as no fixed abode and Paddy Muldoon who, when asked for his address, said, 'I live in the flat above him.'

RC: And thieves in a stolen car were apprehended after a 100 m.p.h. chase by P.C. Wainwright who followed them on foot. Said P.C. Wainwright afterwards, 'I had no choice They shut the door on my truncheon'.

RB: At long last Mario 'Wide-Boy' Minelli was today arrested by the Serious Crimes Squad. He was then chased round the cells with a custard pie by the Silly Crimes Squad.

LATER A MAN WAS CHARGED

RC: A man was charged at Henlade today with ill-treating his wife. She had apparently had so many silicone operations, he was using her to polish the car.

RB: Following an incident in Oxford Street involving three lady shoppers and a policeman's truncheon, Mr. Bert Whizzer, a one-man band, has been charged with conducting himself improperly.

RC: A vicar who rode his bicycle the wrong way up the M6 was asked in court how on earth he managed to avoid an accident. He replied, 'God was with me.' He was further charged with riding two on a bike.

NEWS FROM THE COURTS

RB: The longest ever swearing-in of a witness ended in the High Court this afternoon after 6½ days when the witness, Bert Osby, instead of holding the Bible and reading out the card, held the card and read out the Bible.

RC: Lord Chief Justice Harris today laid down the maximum penalty for bigamy: two mothers-in-law.

CIVIL CASES

RB: An insurance company refused to pay out a claim, stating that the claimant, Mr. Henry Bowker, was blind drunk and smoking in bed. Mr. Bowker won his case when he replied., 'I was not in the least drunk and anyway the bed was alight when I got into it.'

RC: A man who ate an orange contaminated with mercury successfully sued the Moshe McTavish Fruit Co. for injuries. He said every time the temperature went up he hit his head on the ceiling.

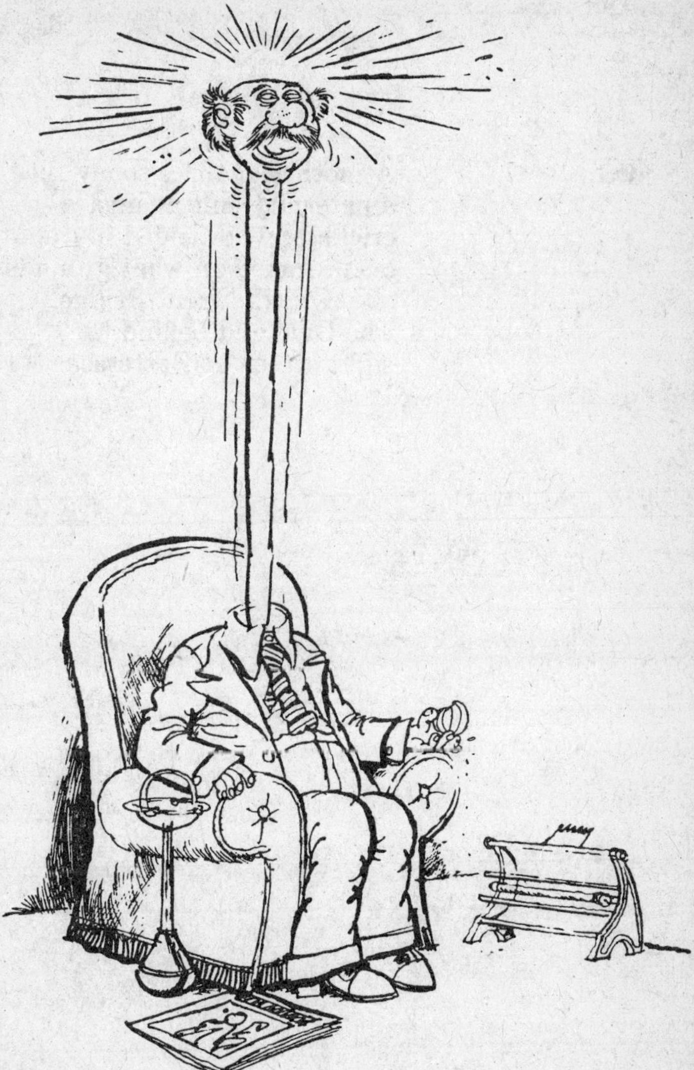

RB: A mother of three today filed a paternity suit against a cricketer who fielded in the deep. Asked on what grounds she replied, 'Trent Bridge, The Oval and behind the sight screen at Battersea Park.'

RC: In the last civil case heard today, a man complained of the noise made by the amorous couple in the flat above him. Each evening they'd sing 'The Red Flag', eat their supper, have fun on the sofa and take a very naughty bath together —

RB: — So every night it was hammer and sickle, cheese and pickle, slap and tickle and bubble and squeak.

UNCIVIL CASES

RC: A man appeared at Bingley Magistrates Court today accused of stealing a hundredweight of curried radishes. Police said that he had swallowed the evidence. He was remanded into custody pending very loud reports.

RB: And the driving instructor who undid a lady's bra whilst giving her a lesson, today had his licence endorsed for exceeding the limits in a built-up area.

RC: A man who broke into Brigitte Bardot's bedroom and laid his hands on her jewellery has been found guilty but insane.

RB: While in the Central Criminal Court a man was acquitted of gross indecency as he'd only been indecent 143 times.

RC: Mr. Henry Gummage, the farm labourer who suffered a serious injury from a reaping machine while dallying in the corn with a young lady, has successfully defended against three paternity suits on the grounds of diminished responsibility.

RB: An unemployed labourer was found guilty of running up and down Downing St. at two o'clock in the morning shouting 'All the Government is barmy!' He was given a two pound fine for being drunk and disorderly and a ten-year gaol sentence for revealing a state secret.

RC: A journalist who slandered the Chancellor of the Exchequer very badly was given a chance to do better in the High Court today.

RB: Whilst at Pirbright Police Station a woman claimed that a squad of cavalrymen from the Light Brigade crept up to her house and seduced her. When asked if she would prefer charges she replied, 'Yes I would. It would be noisy but I wouldn't be kept waiting so long . . .'

RC: And at the Old Bailey, Jim Spraggs, the world's greatest confidence trickster, sentenced the Judge to five years' hard labour.

RB: Thirty drunken trippers who nipped off their coach for a certain reason on Hammersmith Bridge just as the Cambridge crew were sinking underneath have each been fined ten pounds for having one over the eight.

RC: Flann O'Brien and Faustus Kelly were fined at Kilburn Magistrates' Court this morning for causing an affray. Their defence was that they were trying to separate each other.

RB: And in a very serious case in the High Court this afternoon an eighteen-year-old secretary in the Foreign Office confessed that she disgraced herself at an Embassy reception by entertaining a Russian spy on the bedroom carpet, the Mayor of Helsinki in the garbage can, a Chinese attache in the washbasin, a Prussian officer in the fuel receptacle and an African Chief in the downstairs toilet. Summing up, the Judge said she had a Red under the bed, a Finn in the bin, a Chink in the sink, a Junker in the bunker and a Swazi in the khasi . . .

IN THE DIVORCE COURT TODAY...

RC: . . . A husband claimed that his wife's mother kept shouting at him that he was driving too fast along the M1 — and to make matters worse she swore at him while he was untying her from the roof-rack.

RB: And an executive from a toothpaste manufacturing company was divorced by his wife on the grounds of cruelty. She claimed he kept squeezing her the wrong end.

RC: Then Madame Fifi Dubonnet, the former Picasso model, claimed that last Sunday her husband severely assaulted her and gave her three black eyes.

RB: But a sex-crazed lady dietician from Welwyn Garden City admitted in court — 'Yes, there are 263 men in my life . . . and they all eat shredded wheat . . .'

RC: In the next case a husband claimed that he had seen the milkman put his arm round his wife three times. Dismissing the case the Judge said no milkman had an arm that long.

RB: And a Mr. George Thomas was granted a divorce on the grounds of his wife's adultery. After the hearing he stated, 'She led me a dog's life. I was fed on scraps, made to fetch slippers and forced to beg for my favourite biscuits. So when I found her in bed with the postman, I did what anyone else in my position would have done — I bit him in the leg.'

RC: In the next case a traffic light manufacturer was granted a divorce on the grounds that his wife only ever wore three nightdresses; a red one which meant 'Stop — you can't go.' — a flashing yellow one which meant 'You may go, but give way to pedestrians.' and a red and amber one which meant 'You may go only if you have started or are so close to the line that to stop suddenly might cause an accident.'

RB: Another lady, a clairvoyant from Carshalton, was granted a divorce on the grounds of her husband's adultery next weekend in Brighton.

RC: And an 85-year-old farmer divorced his seventeen-year-old wife because he couldn't keep his hands off her. He's now sacked his hands and bought a combine harvester.

RB: Mental cruelty was held as proved in the defended divorce case of Todwick versus Todwick today. Mr. Todwick admitted his wife's accusation that he constantly brought up her poor cooking during conversation.

RC: In an adjacent court Sheikh Haroun el Ramn was being sued for divorce by his 500 wives. It seems they came home early one night last week and caught him with 500 other women.

RB: And a woman from Warrington gained a divorce on the grounds that whenever lightning flashed in the night her husband jumped up shouting 'I'll buy the negatives.'

RC: Later, three men who had failed to keep up with their alimony payments were repossessed by their ex-wives.

RB: In the sketch that follows, I'll be playing a man whose wife left him for the dustman.

RC: And I'll be playing the dustman who refuses to take him.

PRISON ROUND-UP

RB: There was trouble at Pentonville Prison today when a bomb destroyed the toilet block. Local residents have complained that, since then, at least twenty inmates have been seen going over the wall.

RC: And there was a red alert at Dartmoor this morning when it was realised that twenty-six of the prisoners had put their names down for picnic lunches.

RB: Mr. George Thrakes, the building contractor who was gaoled last year for supplying millions of poundsworth of defective building materials to the Government, escaped from Wormwood Scrubs today when the front fell off.

WE'VE JUST HEARD...

RC: . . . That the West Drayton man who kept himself awake every night for seventeen years by snoring, has at last found the answer. He's going to sleep in another room.

RB: We've also heard that a car mounted the kerb outside Mrs. Mary Whitehouse's home this evening so she threw a bucket of water over it.

News from the Church

RC: His Holiness the Pope mingled informally with the crowd in St. Peter's Square today when his balcony collapsed.

RB: Aborigines in the remotest part of Sarawak are having their first taste of Christianity. He was the Reverend J.G. Podmore of Warminster.

RC: While Catholic missionaries in Matabeleland are reporting progress with a tribe of cannibals. They're not completely cured but they are improving. On Fridays they only eat fishermen.

AND NOW FOR TONIGHT'S SPORTS NEWS

Soccer

RB: England's team for the World Cup was finally chosen today. It's Holland.

RC: Fulham F.C., worried by falling attendances, have just paid £90,000 for three spectators from Liverpool.

RB: George Rumford, the Neasden Palace Striker who committed a vicious foul in Saturday's televised game, was today awarded a six match suspension, four for the offence and two for the action replay.

Show Jumping

RC: At the Ladies' Show Jumping, The Hon. Daphne Squire-Pilkington got three faults for a refusal — and Miss Elsie Jones got four pounds for an acceptance.

Yachting

RB: In the Transatlantic single-handed yacht race Mr. Owen Smithers has been disqualified for using both hands.

Athletics

RC: In the International relay event at the White City today, the Irish 4 by 400 metres team built up a commanding lead before handing the baton to the Russian team.

RB: The Finnish girl sprinter, Hella Lundquist, went home today, well pleased after completing 100 laps round Helsinki Stadium for charity. So did the 100 Lapps.

RC: After this incident, reports that athletes indulge in too much sex before meetings were hotly denied by sprinter Wellesley Blunt. He went on to win the hundred metres in a time of two hours thirty seven minutes.

RB: Furthermore, at Crystal Palace this evening, Neville Stitch broke his own world record in the eight hundred metres. He was so pleased he went on to try the high hurdles, but, thinking they were the low hudles, he shattered his personal best.

RC: Finally, it's been revealed in a report laid before the International Olympic Committee that at the last Olympic games several athletes took steroids, the Russian gymnast Anna Volga took annaroids, Anthony Armstrong-Jones took several polaroids and David Hemery took syrup of figs.

Racing

RB: Champion jockey Ainsley Beasley was injured at Waverley today. He received a black eye when Racquel Welch turned round too quickly to say hello.

RC: It was a lucky day again for Honest Jack Duggan, the bookie cum sex maniac. He made indecent suggestions to ten girls during the 3.30 at Sandown Park — only three ran.

RB: Earlier, Duggan was in court, charged with seducing a young lady at Bechers Brook. He asked for 26 other fences to be taken into consideration.

Cycling

RC: There's news from Japan that Mr. Watanabe Akimoto, the winner of the slow bicycle race in the 1972 Olympics, has just completed his lap of honour.

Mountaineering

RB: Mountaineers using the new elastic rope on Kanchenjunga report one great advantage. If you do happen to slip you finish on a higher ledge than the one you fell from.

Tug-of-war

RC: Tonight's tug-of-war between England and France my have to be cancelled if nobody can find a twenty-six mile rope.

Greyhound Racing

RB: Stewards tonight called off the greyhound meeting at Killarney after tests revealed that somebody had drugged the hare.

Aerobatics

RC: At the Royal Air Show today, Luigi Bregonzi, the famous drunken Italian air ace, was not permitted to do his celebrated dive through the sound barrier. The controller said he could not endanger the crown with a high tiddley iteye boom boom!

Tennis

RB: The draw for next year's Wimbledon Doubles Championship was made tonight. There will be a confused opening round in which a woman, and a man who used to be a woman, meet a man and a woman who used to be a man. The winners of that match will play a man who became a woman but is now a man again, partnered by a woman who's saving up to be a ballboy.

And there's just time to tell you...

RC: . . . That George Mumble, the Home Counties' Most Henpecked Husband died today. By the terms of his will, his ashes will be scattered all over his wife's new living-room carpet.

RB: And we've just heard a heartwarming story of coincidence. Mrs. Fanny Hughes was born on the fifteenth of the month, christened on the 15th, met her husband-to-be on the 15th, married on the 15th and spent her 15 day honeymoon in room 15. Now she's run off with the Aberavon Rugby Team.

RC: Another piece of late news. Mr. Arthur Perkiss, the man who this week won £500,000 on the pools, has announced that he will never work another day in his life. So he's staying on with British Rail.

RB: Here is a news flash just come in: Milk bottles were thrown at a meeting of the Milk Marketing Board this afternoon and a meeting of the Egg Marketing Board was also broken up when eggs were thrown. A mass meeting of the Manure Marketing Board has been cancelled.

RC: Reports are also coming in that an elephant has done the ton on the M1. Motorists are advised to use great caution and treat it as a roundabout.

RB: Finally, though, let us remind you that the new BBC series 'How to Improve Your Sex Life' goes out for the first time tonight at 11.45. And just in case you miss it, it will be repeated at twenty minute intervals throughout the night.

Well, That's All For This Week. Next Week We'll Be Talking To....

RC: . . . A man who was imprisoned in Wormwood Scrubs for his beliefs. He believed the night watchman was asleep.

RB: And to Albert Nudge, a retired goldfish breeder, who's been appointed head of a committee to solve the pollution problem in the English Channel. He's already told the government that they'll have to see that the water's changed three times a week.

RC: And to two politicians, one of whom says he wouldn't mind a bit if more women were in power. Whilst the other says he wouldn't mind a bit and doesn't care who's in power.

RB: And to the superstitious doctor who won't ever ask for a specimen on St. Swithin's Day.

RC: Then we'll be meeting the Runcorn woman who married a Gas Board fitter and complains that on her wedding night three of them turned up — one to estimate the job, one to do it and one to pick up the bits in the morning.

RB: And the well-known Court photographer who'll be showing us some of the photos he managed to get before he was caught.

RC: And that famous order of bionic nuns — the Little Transistors of the Poor.

RB: Then as a rehearsal for his role in 'Stars On Sunday' Lester Piggott will read the sermon on the mount.

RC: And I'll be reviewing a book that's just become a best-seller in Scotland, entitled 'Indoor Games for Flag Days'.

RB: Then by way of light relief we'll be taking a look at fur-covered toilet seats and asking: do they tickle your fancy?

RC: And for sports fans there'll be rugby with Eddie Waring, boxing with Eddie Tiring and archaeology with Eddie Downright-Boring.

RB: Then we've got a rather unusual snake charming act featuring the world's most ancient performing reptiles. The act is called Abdul and his Load of Old Cobras.

RC: And for culture lovers we'll have an excerpt from the new Grand Opera, 'Eskimo Nell' — in which a seventeen stone contralto sings 'You're Tiny . . . And it's Frozen . . .'

RB: And there's a choice for you lady sports fans, either football with David Coleman, snooker with David Gasman, or hanky-panky with David Milkman.

RC: Lastly we'll visit tonight's big charity ball in which well-known personalities will be doing the things that have made them famous. Jimmy Tarbuck will be telling jokes, Pam Ayres will recite some poems, Uri Geller will ruin the cutlery and Christopher Lee will strangle a waiter.

I'VE JUST BEEN HANDED A PIECE OF PAPER...

RB: ... It says, a chemist's shop in Eastbourne was broken into last night. The entire stock was taken except for quantities of hair cream and the pill. Police are looking for a bald headed Catholic.

RC: But that is certainly all there's room for in this selection. Hope you've enjoyed it. But now it's goodbye from me.

RB: And it's goodbye from him.

BOTH: Goodbye.

The mysterious writer who supplies the news items to 'The Two Ronnies' works under several aliases. Can you guess which of the following is his real name?

Alec Adcock, Peter Bain, Alec Baron, John Bartlett, Norman Beedle, Robert Belford, Dennis Berson, Ray Binns, George Brodie and Mike Perry, Alex Brown and Pat Murray, Mary Butcher, Peter Campbell and Roger Ordish, Philip Campbell and Myron Edwards, Stuart Campbell, Garry Chambers, Syd Clark, Mike Cole and John McGrouther, John Cotterill, Barry Cryer, Manny Curtis, Tommy Desmond, Graham Deykin, Dixon and Wallis, Malcolm Drew, Dave Dutton, Pete Edwards, Stan Edwards, Wyn Edwards, Paul Eldergill, Harry Evans, Derek Farmer, Eric Flitcroft, Ernest Forbes, Cathie Foote, Fuzz, Phil Gould, Neville Gurnhill, Stephen Hancocks, Tony Hare, Tony Hawes, Bob Hedley, Frank Hickman, Les Higgins, Tim Hopkins, Howard Imber, John Irving, Desmond Jones, Tudor Jones, S.C. Kidd, Dorothy Kilmurry-Hall, Frank Kirkbride,

Gary Knight, Les Lilley, John Lloyd, Roy Lomax, Ray Lowry, David McKellar, Tom Magee-Englefield, Malcolm Mather, Tony Mather, Wally Malston, Wally McKinley, Fred Metcalf, Mike Meys, Chris Miller, Philip Munnoch, Alex Miles, Ralph Morris, David Newman, Anthony Nicholson, David Nobbs, Wendy Norton, Gavin Osbon, Tony Payne, Jon Peat, Terry Ravenscroft, Keith Rawnsley and Pete Long, David Renwick, Tony Rich, Peter Robinson, Kenneth Rock, Laurie Rowley, John Sayle, Robert Scott, Les Scott, Eric Searle, Neil Shand, Charles Shiells, Robin Soans, Austin Steele, Tony Stevens, Gordon Stretch, Hugh Stuckey, John Sullivan, Edward Taylor, Terry Treloar, Dick Vosburgh, Len Walker, David Webb, Ron Weighell, Alan Wightman, Gerald Wiley and Stan Wootton.

HUMOUR

0352	396954	Harry Secombe **GOON FOR LUNCH**	60p
	39899X	Peter Vincent **THE TWO RONNIES: BUT FIRST THE NEWS**	60p
	301082	**MORE OF THE TWO RONNIES: NICE TO BE WITH YOU AGAIN!**	60p
	30152X	P.G. Wodehouse **A DAMSEL IN DISTRESS**	75p
	301503	**A GENTLEMAN OF LEISURE**	75p
	301694	**SOMETHING FISHY**	75p
0426		Universal/Tandem	
	186494	Christopher Kenworthy **CITIZEN SMITH**	70p ♦
	157982	Spike Milligan **A BOOK OF BITS**	50p
	158199	**THE LITTLE POTBOILER**	50p
	15827X	**A DUSTBIN OF MILLIGAN**	50p
	157710	**THE BEDSIDE MILLIGAN**	50p
	158008	**THE BEDSITTING ROOM**	50p
0427		Trophy	
	002036	Roger Brook, (Editor) **REALLY NURSE! and WAKE UP NURSE!**	50p
	002044	**AND AFTER THAT NURSE?**	40p
	002052	B. Kliban **CAT**	95p*

† For sale in Britain and Ireland only.
* Not for sale in Canada.
♦ Film & T.V. tie-ins.